Sushi Cookbook

For Beginners

A Simple Guide To Making Sushi At Home With
Over 70 Delicious Sushi Recipes

KRISTEN BARTON

ISBN-13: 978-1518892387

ISBN-10: 1518892388

DEDICATION

To Trevor, for teaching me how to enjoy more of the hiding treasures of life.

TABLE OF CONTENT

Read Other Books By Kristen Barton:

Delicious Homemade Jerky Recipes: 43 Jerky Recipes For Easy
Meal Times - Beef Jerky, Chicken Jerky, Turkey Jerky, Fish Jerky,
Venison Jerky And More

Foraging For Beginners: A Simple Foragers Guide To Wild Edible
Plants And Medicinal Herbs

INTRODUCTION

The popularity of sushi has grown immensely in Western countries over the past few years. Once you've tried a little spicy tuna roll, it is almost impossible not to fall in love with this distinctly unique part of Asian cuisine. Once you've had your first taste, it is very likely you will want another, and another.. And one day, you may want to embark on the culinary adventure of making your first sushi.

The most common sushi consists of rice shaped into patties or mounds and topped with raw fish or rolled with fish, roe and vegetables wrapped in seaweed. There are many forms available to choose from when deciding on sushi. There is rolled sushi, pressed sushi, bowl sushi, sushi in a pocket and sushi by itself. The main ingredient in sushi is rice, in different forms with a variety of fish and vegetables, which gives it a distinctive taste. The same

1

ingredients can be formed in several different ways to create different forms of sushi.

Variations of sushi have made their way to the Western World. What once was pure crab meat used in sushi dishes is now imitation crab meat. The crab meat is tasty however. Beef and chicken are used in some of the sushi dishes, and even some dishes utilize spam, an unknown meat source. Imagination can run wild when creating new dishes.

There are also other variations of sushi. There is Latin sushi, which uses a lot of different spices with a Latino flavor. There is Caribbean sushi also, which utilizes tropical spices and fruits. The Mediterranean Sushi takes on a different flavor. A lot of feta cheese, olives and other spices are used in these. There are many different areas that create their own sushi with their own spices and flavors. Enjoy original sushi or sushi of the area you are in. It is worth your time. You will be able to make many types at home with the recipes in this book. Experiment with different forms and types of sushi. Enjoy the dipping sauces and the wonderful flavor of the pickled ginger. Your palate will praise you for choosing this enticing, delectable form of food.

Incorporate these forms of sushi to be served as a cozy meal for 2 or a meal for several. Have a sushi tasting get together with friends or co-workers. There are surely ones among your circle that have never tried sushi and you can be the one to introduce them. Make sure there are several choices of sushi and several sides to tempt their palate. Don't forget the wasabi and pickled ginger.

Making your own sushi at home will accomplish a number of things for you. One is that you will save a good amount of money. We all know that the sushi you get from sushi bars and Japanese restaurants are often overpriced. The second is the sense of accomplishment that comes with "mastering" this special part of Asian cuisine. Not only will you gain personal satisfaction for being able to prepare this dish, you will also impress your friends and family with the huge variety of homemade sushi you have expertly crafted.

You don't have to be a world class chef to make sushi at home. It is within your grasp as long as you have the basic kitchen skills of combining ingredients. All you need to do is cook some rice, get some nori, slice some fish and vegetables and then roll them all together! Your first few tries may not end as lovely as you expected. Rolls will be uneven, rice will be loosely packed and some ingredients may fall out. However, with a lot of practice, you will get the presentation right and you will soon start making lovely and elegant sushi right in your own home. Below is a guide for making your own sushi at home.

Beginners Guide To Making Sushi At Home

1. Know The Different Sushi Presentation Styles

Sushi is presented in different styles and you will prefer some to others. Here are the common types of sushi:

−*Makizushi (Sushi Rolls):* This includes

Chumaki (medium roll sushi),

Futomaki (thick roll sushi that has several fillings),

Hosomaki (thin roll sushi with a single filling),

Temaki (hand roll with a cone shape) and

Uramaki (inside-out roll sushi that has nori on the inside and rice on outside)

–Nigirizushi (Hand-Formed Sushi): This consist of sushi rice hand formed into a rectangle with a slice of fish or seafood on top

–Chirashizushi (Scattered Sushi): This consist of a bowl with sushi rice topped with sliced raw fish and often with vegetables.

–Inarizushi (Sushi Wrapped In Something That Is Not Nori): This is usually sushi ingredients wrapped in tofu pouches.

–Oshizushi (Pressed Sushi): This is sushi that is made and pressed into wooden molds. The rectangular box of sushi is then cut into smaller rectangles or squares before serving.

–Sashimi: This is just raw fish or seafood served without sushi rice.

2. Get The Necessary Equipment

The right tools will make it easier for you to make sushi at home. Here are the basic tools you require:

–Rice cooker: A rice cooker has a consistent cooking process and provides more convenience because you don't have to constantly watch or stir. On the other hand, if you do not want to commit to a rice cooker immediately, you can use a plain old non-stick cooking pot that has a lid.

– Sushi-grade knives: The sushi knife is nice to have to help you slice your sashimi and creating the art. They are extremely sharp which helps to create a nice smooth appearance. You need a few sharp knifes for cutting fish, veggies and sushi rolls. Basically, you should have a heavy chef's knife with a curved blade, a long slim and very sharp fish knife that will also double for sushi rolls and lastly a knife that you will use to peel, cut and chop vegetables.

– Rice rolling mat (bamboo): The ultimate must have is a bamboo mat. The art of rolling maki is a lot easier when you have this mat. It helps when pressing and forming the roll.

– *Plastic wrap:* To keep rice from sticking to the rolling mat. It also prolongs the life of the mat since you will not have to wash it too frequently.

– **Large wooden mixing bowl***:* A hangiri (Japanese round, flat-bottomed bowl) is helpful in mixing rice with your seasonings for sushi rice. This is needed for mixing as well as cutting sushi rice. You could also use a plastic bowl.

– *Wooden spoon or rice paddle:* You need this for "cutting" sushi rice. Rice paddles are better to use with your rice cooker instead of your regular utensils. The non-stick surfaces are safe with a rice paddle.

– *Small plates and bowls:* For serving and lining up ingredients.

– *Cutting board*

– *Colander*

– *Large bowl:* To wash rice and vegetables

– *Others:* A sushi mold helps to create the pressed sushi. It is quicker when using the mold than forming by hand. To create the full sushi effect, you need the serving dishes and utensils. There are sushi platters, plates, boats and of course, the chopsticks. This completes a full stock of needed items for making sushi and for serving sushi.

3. Assemble Your Ingredients

Sushi ingredients are many but you don't have to buy all of them to begin making sushi at home. The list below includes the basic ingredients to get you started. A few optional ingredients are also listed. Combinations of all of these ingredients enhance the flavors of the dish you are preparing.

You will get the best results only when you have the right ingredients. Pay attention to the rice and fish as they are the most important ingredients. Sushi grade fish is quite costly but it is vital to use the proper grade for the best taste and your safety. Many of the ingredients are available in standard grocery stores but you may have to visit Asian food stores for others.

– Sushi rice: The best sushi rice is the short-grained type. It has the right stickiness because it is starchy and absorbent. If you use Basmati or another long-grained type, it will be too dry and hard. Check the packaging to make sure that it is clearly labeled "sushi rice". The best selections are usually available at the local Asian market.

– Sushi grade fish and seafood: There are certain characteristics that will help you to identify sushi-grade fish. Choose fish that is firm and smooth to the touch and not slimy. It must be bright colored, not dark or dull. It should not smell. The presence of a strong smell means the fish is old. Buy fillets rather than steaks, because they are easier to slice for sushi.

There are many types of sushi grade fish. Two of the most popular are salmon and tuna. Others include eel, squid, octopus, shrimp, mackerel, crab, scallops, red snapper and roe from salmon or smelt. Other meats besides fish can be used also. This has become more popular as sushi migrated to America. Ocean fish is the only fish that can be served raw. Fresh water fish needs to be cooked to make sure parasites are killed. Raw fish needs to be fresh for sushi, which you can tell by color and smell.

– Rice vinegar (komezu): Rice vinegar is used along with sugar and salt to season sushi rice. This seasoning is what gives sushi rice its sweet and tart flavor.

– Kombu: This is a dried seaweed used to add flavor to sushi rice. It is added to the pot when cooking rice.

– Sake: This is a Japanese rice wine that is crucial to the taste of sushi rice. Additionally, it possesses anti-bacterial properties that serves as a preservative.

– Wasabi: This is Japanese horseradish that is available in the form of a powder or paste. It can be added to the top of the rice or the soy sauce for dipping.

– *Soy Sauce:* This is used as an ingredients and also as dipping sauce.

– *Kewpie (Japanese mayonnaise)*

– *Nori (seaweed wrap):* Another important ingredient to use is seaweed. Good quality nori is black and not green. It is in many recipes, especially the rolled sushi. It can be used as garnishment as well as forming the rolls, making it easier to eat.

– *Sushi ginger:* This pickled ginger is usually placed in the corner of a sushi tray. It is eaten after sushi to cleanse the palate.

– *Crab meat (real or imitation)*

– *Green tea (Ocha):* In Japan, green tea is traditionally served with sushi. It is used for refreshing the mouth before eating and also between bites. It also helps to douse the wasabi burn if it is too "hot" for you. You can buy regular, coarse or powdered green tea.

– *Sushi Vegetables:* Vegetables and fruits are used also in sushi. The can range from avocados, snow peas, asparagus, mangos, strawberries, cucumber, carrots, onions, lettuce, daikon radishes and shitake mushrooms. There are many others that can be incorporated into the recipes. Experimenting with taste combinations is good in sushi.

4. Preparing Your First Sushi

Step 1 – Cook The Rice (Basic Sushi Rice Recipe)

Preparation Time: 5 minutes

Cooking Time: 20 minutes

Servings: 4

Ingredients:

Uncooked sushi rice, 3 cups

Water, 3 1/4 cups

Kombu, 1 sheet

Rice vinegar, 1/3 cup

Sugar, 4 Tbsp.

Salt, 2 tsp.

Directions:

Rice Cooker Preparation

1. Before cooking, wash the rice with cold water, swirling with your hands to remove any bran or powder. Rinse with fresh water 4-5times until no longer cloudy.

2. Add rice and water to the rice maker, place the kombu on top then set the time to start cooking.

3. Meanwhile, combine sugar, salt and rice vinegar in a small sauce pan. Stir the mixture on low heat until sugar and salt are dissolved completely. Set aside to cool.

4. When rice is done, transfer to a large wooden bowl.

5. Sprinkle the vinegar mixture, a little at a time all over the rice. Use a wooden spoon to make cutting motions across the rice and scoop from bottom to top as you sprinkle so that each grain is coated. Fan the rice with a piece of newspaper while mixing in the vinegar mixture. When you are done, the rice should be shiny and sticky and "just warm" not cold or hot.

Stove Top Preparation

1. Add the rice and water to a saucepan and top with the kombu.

2. Cover with lid and bring to a boil on high heat. Reduce to low heat then cook for 20 minutes.

3. Follow steps number 3-5 (above) to complete the preparation.

Step 2 – Slice Vegetables

Julienne or thinly slice the cucumbers, carrots, avocado and crab meat. You can use a slicer or simply slice by hand. Slice as thinly as possible to get thin long strips. Place each ingredient in a small bowl.

Step 3 – Slice The Fish

Place the fish fillet flat on the cutting board. Starting from the left side, hold the knife so that you will cut against the grain. Cut straight down, pulling towards you and slice through each time. If you want an angled cut, simply angle the knife's blunt edge to the right. Cut thin slices, about 1/8 inch. Continue slicing from left to right until the entire fillet is sliced. Sushi fish can be cut in the following five basic ways.

–The rectangular cut is very simple and is the most common. You can use it for all fish.

– Use a cube cut for soft thick fish.

– The angled cut is usually used for nagiri.

– If the fish is firm, you can use a paper-thin cut.

– The thread cut is usually used for thin white fish fillets and squid.

Step 4 – Wrap And Roll Your Sushi

Start by mixing 2-3 tablespoons of vinegar with 1 cup of water in a bowl. Dip your hands in this solution while assembling the sushi. This will stop rice from sticking to your hands.

Spread out the bamboo mat and cover it with plastic wrap (saran). Place a half sheet of nori with the shiny face down on the plastic wrap. (The way you place the nori does not matter when making an inside out roll.)

Dip your hands in the vinegar water then grab some sushi rice (about 3/4 cup). Spread a layer of rice (about ¼ inch thick) on the bottom three-quarters of the nori sheet. Leave the top one-quarter of the sheet empty for sealing the roll together. Spread evenly then press the rice down so that it sticks to the nori sheet.

Make a horizontal groove along the length of the rice. Place a thin layer of ingredients (usually 3 or 5 items, depending on your recipe) like vegetables, fish or crab meat on top of the groove you made.

Add a little swipe of wasabi on top or pour any sauce you want to use such as Japanese mayonnaise.

To roll the sushi (with rice on the inside):

Place the tips of the 4 fingers of both hands on the ingredients to hold them down and each thumb under the bamboo (see picture above).

Start rolling gradually and firmly until the mat goes around completely and the top edge of the nori meets the bottom edge. Pull out your fingers and complete the roll to make a tight cylinder. Squeeze firmly but don't press too hard.

Unroll the mat, and your first sushi roll is ready. Place it on a plate and make additional rolls. Before cutting, let the sushi rolls set for some minutes to enable the rice and ingredients stick together.

To cut the sushi roll:

Place a sushi roll on the cutting board. Use a sharp knife to cut the roll in half (wet the knife first). Then cut the two halves in half again and finally the four halves in half. This gives you 8 bite-sized pieces. Repeat for the remaining sushi rolls and arrange on a plate.

Making An Inside Out Sushi Roll:

Spread out the bamboo mat and cover it with plastic wrap (saran). Place a half sheet of nori on the plastic wrap.

Wet your fingers in the vinegar water then grab some sushi rice (about 3/4 cup). Spread a layer of rice on the entire nori surface. Spread evenly then press the rice down so that it sticks to the nori sheet.

Place a piece of plastic wrap on the rice and flip so that the nori is facing up. Now add your ingredients on the nori at the bottom of the sheet.

Use the same hand position as the regular sushi and roll until the two edges of the sushi come together. Continue to roll, applying necessary pressure until the mat is completely around the sushi roll.

Remove the mat and plastic wrap and place the sushi roll on a plate. Decorate the outside with fish roe or toasted sesame seeds. Lastly, cut as described above.

5. Eating Your First Sushi

When eating sushi at home, you are allowed some flexibility. You can use chop sticks or your fingers.

Eat bite-sized sushi in one bite. Don't overuse wasabi or soy sauce. A dab of wasabi or a sparing dip in soy sauce is all you need to provide the right compliment to the flavor of the sushi.

MAKI SUSHI RECIPES (Rolled Sushi)

Dragon Roll Recipe

Preparation Time: 1 hour

Cooking Time: 0

Servings: 4

Ingredients:

Sushi rice, 6 cups

Japanese cucumber, 1

Avocados, 4 small

Nori sheets, 4

Shrimp tempura, 16, precooked

Tobiko, 1/8 cup

Eel, optional

Spicy mayonnaise

Unagi (eel) Sauce

Sesame Seeds, black

Water, ¼ cup

Rice vinegar, 2 Tsp.

Directions:

1. Slice cucumber into long strips. Throw the seeds away.

2. Peel the avocado, remove the seed and slice across into strips.

3. Press the avocado with fingers until same length as cucumber. Sprinkle with lemon juice.

4. Spread your bamboo mat with plastic. Place 1/2 nori sheet on plastic. Mix vinegar and water. Dip hands in water mixture.

5. Spread the rice onto the nori sheet.

6. Turn the sheet with rice over and place shrimp tempura, cucumbers and tobiko at the bottom of nori sheet. You may also put the eel here also.

7. Hold the bottom end of bamboo mat, roll nori sheet over the filling firmly. Lift mat and roll over.

8. Squeeze the roll tightly with the bamboo mat. Release the mat and place the roll on the bamboo mat.

9. Lay the avocado slices over the roll.

10. Using the bamboo mat, place over plastic wrapped roll and squeeze until avocado wraps around the roll.

11. Cut into 8 slices. Remove plastic and place on serving dish.

12. Spread tobiko on top, sprinkle with spicy mayo and unagi sauce and sesame seeds.

Easy Maki Sushi

Preparation Time: 30 minutes

Cooking Time: 0

Servings: 4

Ingredients:

Sushi rice, 2 cups uncooked

Water, 3 cups

Rice vinegar, 4 Tbsp.

Sugar, 2 Tbsp.

Salt, ½ tsp.

Nori Sheets

Crab Sticks, cooked

Japanese Cucumber, 1

Spicy Mayo, ¼ cup

Directions:

1. Wash and drain rice. Add rice and water to rice cooker and follow times of rice cooker.

2. Combine rice vinegar, sugar and salt. Mix well.

3. Fold vinegar mixture into hot rice. Set aside to cool.

4. Spread plastic wrap onto bamboo mat.

5. Place nori sheet on bamboo mat. Cover the nori sheet with the rice mixture, leaving ½ inch at the bottom.

6. Arrange crab sticks and cucumbers on top of rice. Spread with spicy mayo.

7. Use the bamboo mat to roll the sushi tightly, then squeeze firmly.

8. Slice into 8 slices and serve.

Unagi Roll

Preparation Time: 1 hour

Cooking Time: 15 minutes

Servings: 2 to 4

Ingredients:

Sushi Rice, 4 cups, cooked

Nori sheets, 1 pkg.

Salmon, ½ lb., sliced into strips

Unagi (eel), 1 lb., sliced into strips

Masago, 8 tbsps.

Avocado, 1 peeled and pitted, sliced

Wasabi

Pickled ginger

Sesame seeds, toasted

Eel Sauce:

Soy sauce, 6 Tbsp.

Mirin, 4 Tbsp.

Brown Sugar, 2 Tbsp.

Rice vinegar, 1/8 tsp.

Directions:

1. Prepare your eel sauce first. Mix soy sauce, mirin, brown sugar and rice vinegar. Let boil for 1 minute, then simmer for 5 minutes or until thickened.

2. Place nori sheet on plastic wrap. Spread with sushi rice and press firmly. Leave ½ inch clear at the end of the nori sheet.

3. Flip the nori sheet over. Place salmon, avocado and masago onto nori sheet that has no rice.

4. Using bamboo mat roll the nori sheet tightly beginning at the end with no rice. Shape into roll with plastic wrap still on.

5. Heat the eel in oven for about 10 minutes and layer on top of the rice roll. Press firmly using a bamboo mat.

6. Slice into 8 to 10 pieces, depending on preferred size.

7. Spread roll with eel sauce. Sprinkle with sesame seeds.

8. Serve with soy sauce, wasabi and ginger.

Spicy Tuna Roll

Preparation Time: 1 hour

Cooking Time: 20 minutes

Servings: 4 to 6

Ingredients:

Sushi Rice, 5 cups

Nori Sheets, 1 sheet

Rice Vinegar, ½ cup

Sugar, 4 Tbsp.

Salt, 1 tsp.

Spicy Mayonnaise, 1/2 cup

Sriracha Sauce, ½ tsp.

Chile Sesame Oil, 1 tsp.

Masago, 1 Tbsp.

Chili Powder, ¼ tsp.

Sashimi Tuna, 1 lb., minced

Cucumber, 1 sliced

Avocado, 1 sliced

Directions:

1. Wash rice in 4 changes of water. Place rice in cooker with water and cook approximately 20 minutes.

2. Boil rice vinegar.

3. Add salt and sugar to rice vinegar. Allow to cool.

4. Transfer rice to a mixing bowl. Add the cooled vinegar mixture gradually and turn over with wooden paddle. Set aside to cool, turning occasionally.

5. Mix mayo, sriracha sauce, chili powder, chili sesame oil and masago. Save some for dipping. Add tuna to the mixture and toss to coat.

6. Place plastic wrap on bamboo mat then add nori sheet. Wet fingers then spread nori sheet with sushi rice and press firmly, covering the entire surface with rice.

7. Flip the nori sheet over so that it is now facing up and rice side is under.

8. Layer nori sheet with tuna, avocado and cucumber. Spread with mayo mixture.

7. Roll carefully and firmly, pressing as you go.

8. Slice and serve with soy sauce and mayo mixture.

Cucumber Avocado Maki

Preparation Time: 1 hour

Cooking Time: 15 minutes

Servings: 2

Ingredients:

Sushi Rice, 1 ¼ cup

Water, 1 ½ cup

Salt, ¼ tsp.

Mirin, 2 Tbsp.

Rice Vinegar, 2 Tbsp.

Ginger, 1 small bit, peeled and minced

Avocado, 1 peeled, pitted and sliced

English Cucumber, 1 peeled, seeds removed and sliced

Lime, 1 wedge squeezed

Red Cabbage, 1 head, diced

Wasabi Powder, 2 tsp.

Sesame Oil, 2 Tbsp.

Miso Paste, 1 Tbsp.

Sugar, 1 tsp.

Salt, ¼ tsp.

Pepper, ¼ tsp.

Soy Sauce, ¼ cup

Nori Sheets, 4 sheets

Pickled Ginger, 2 oz.

Sesame Seeds, 1 tsp.

Directions:

1. Prepare vegetables and set aside.

2. Prepare sushi rice with salt and water. Simmer 15 minutes. Let stand 5 minutes, then add mirin and rice vinegar.

3. Spread rice to cool.

4. Mix wasabi powder with 1 tsp. water. Make a paste. Add miso paste, sesame oil, ginger paste, sugar, ½ of the soy sauce and juice of 1 lime wedge.

5. Mix cabbage and the vinaigrette and toss to coat. Add salt and pepper.

6. Lay nori sheet over plastic wrap on bamboo mat, wet fingers and spread rice, leaving a 1-inch edge of sheet clear.

7. Place avocado and cucumber strips in the center of each sheet.

8. Roll tightly and seal with wet fingers.

9. Slice rolls in 6 pieces and sprinkle with sesame seeds.

10. Serve with wasabi paste, ginger, cabbage and soy sauce.

Crab Maki Sushi

Preparation Time: 1 hour

Cooking Time: 15 minutes

Servings: 4

Ingredients:

Sushi Rice, 2 ½ cups

Water, 2 ½ cups cold

Rice Vinegar, 4 Tbsp.

Sugar, 3 Tbsp.

Salt, 2 tsp.

Crab, 10 oz., cut into thin strips

Avocado, 1 peeled, pitted and cut into strips.

Mayonnaise, 2 Tbsp.

Nori, 6 sheets

Soy Sauce, ¼ cup

Pickled ginger, ½ cup

Wasabi Paste, 2 Tbsp.

Directions:

1. Rinse rice, place rice and water in saucepan. Bring to a boil, reduce and simmer for 15 minutes. Remove from heat and let set.

2. Mix vinegar, salt and sugar. Sprinkle mixture over rice and mix.

3. Combine crab meat and mayonnaise, set aside.

4. Lay out Nori sheets over plastic wrap on bamboo mat, wet fingers and press a firm layer of rice onto the sheet, leaving an inch edge.

5. Place a thin line of wasabi paste in the middle of rice.

6. Add crab mixture with slices of avocado on top.

7. Roll firmly, pressing as you go to form the roll.

8. Slice into 1 ½ inch slices. Place on plate.

9. Serve with soy sauce, ginger and wasabi paste.

Tofu And Vegetable Maki Sushi

Preparation Time: 1 hour

Cook Time: 15 minutes

Serves: 4 to 6

Ingredients:

Sushi Rice, 2 ½ cups

Water, 2 ½ cups, cold

Rice Vinegar, 4 Tbsp.

Sugar, 3 Tbsp.

Salt, 2 tsp.

Tofu, 6 ½ oz. firm, cut into strips

Carrot, 1 small, peeled and grated

Shitake mushrooms, 6 , stems removed and thinly sliced

Snow pea sprouts, ½ cup, washed and drained

Nori Sheets, 4

Wasabi Paste, 2 Tbsp.

Soy Sauce, ¼ cup

Pickled ginger, ¼ cup

Directions:

1. Prepare sushi rice with cold water. Bring to boil, reduce and simmer 15 minutes. Cover and set aside.

2. Combine rice vinegar, sugar and salt. Mix well and add to rice.

3. Lay Nori sheets over plastic wrap on bamboo mat.

4. Wet fingers and press rice firmly in a thin layer on Nori sheets, leaving a 1 inch edge.

5. Place tofu strips, carrot, shitake mushroom and snow pea sprouts on top of rice.

6. Begin rolling tightly pressing firmly to form roll.

7. Slice in 1 inch round slices. Place on plate.

8. Serve with wasabi paste, soy sauce and pickled ginger.

NIGIRIZUSHI RECIPES (Hand-pressed Sushi)

Salmon Nigiri

Preparation Time: 45 minutes

Cook Time: 15 minutes

Servings: 4

Ingredients:

Sushi Rice, 2 cups

Water, 2 ¼ cups, cold

Rice vinegar, ½ cup

Sugar, 2 Tbsp.

Salt, ½ tsp.

Sashimi grade salmon, 1 lb., sliced into strips

Wasabi Paste, ¼ cup

Soy Sauce, ¼ cup

Pickled ginger, ½ cup

Directions:

1. Soak rice in water and drain until water runs clear.

2. Combine rice and water and bring to a boil over medium heat. Reduce heat and simmer 15 minutes.

3. Mix rice vinegar, sugar and salt. Drizzle over rice and combine with wooden spoon gently.

4. Form rice into an oval shape on wood surface.

5. Place salmon slices on top of rice and press firmly.

6. Serve with pickled ginger, soy sauce and wasabi paste.

7. Add a nice tea to complete meal.

Mackerel Nigirishuhi

Preparation Time: 45 minutes

Cooking Time: 20

Serves: 4

Ingredients:

Sushi Rice, 2 cups

Water, 2 cups

Rice Vinegar, 3 Tbsp.

Sugar, 2 Tbsp.

Salt, 1 tsp.

Mackerel, 1 lb., sliced

Wasabi Paste, ¼ cup

Soy Sauce, ½ cup

Pickled Ginger, ¼ cup

Directions:

1. Cook rice with water in rice cooker for 20 minutes. Let sit 10 minutes.

2. Combine rice vinegar, sugar, salt and water. Add to rice and blend lightly.

3. Wet fingers and form rice into rectangular pats.

4. Spread a thin layer of wasabi paste on top of rice pat.

5. Add a slice of mackerel and press lightly.

6. Serve with soy sauce and pickled ginger.

Bonito Nigirizushi

Preparation Time: 40 minutes

Cooking Time: 20 minutes

Serves: 4

Ingredients:

Sushi Rice, 2 cups

Water, 2 cups

Rice Vinegar, 3 Tbsp.

Sugar, 3 Tbsp.

Salt, 1 tsp.

Bonito Fillets, 1 lb., sliced

Avocado, 1 peeled, pitted and sliced thin

Soy Sauce, ¼ cup

Wasabi Paste, ¼ cup

Pickled Ginger, ¼ cup

Directions:

1. Rinse rice and drain until water is clear.

2. Cook rice with water in rice cooker for 20 minutes. Let stand for 10 minutes.

3. Mix rice vinegar, sugar and salt together. Pour over sushi rice and mix lightly.

4. Wet fingers and form rice into rectangular pats.

5. Spread thin line of wasabi paste down the middle of the rice pat.

6. Place slice of avocado and a slice of bonito. Continue with the rest and form pats.

7. Serve with soy sauce and pickled ginger.

Tuna Nigirizushi

Preparation Time: 45 minutes

Cooking Time: 15 minutes

Servings: 4

Ingredients:

Sushi Rice, 2 ½ cups

Water, 2 cups

Rice vinegar, 2 Tbsp.

Sugar, 2 Tbsp.

Salt,1 tsp.

Tuna Slices, 1 lb.

Soy Sauce, ½ cup

Wasabi Paste, ¼ cup

Pickled Ginger, ½ cup

Directions:

1. Clean rice in cold water and drain until water runs clear.

2. Cook rice in water over medium heat for 15 minutes, let stand.

3. Mix rice vinegar, sugar and salt. Sprinkle over rice and fold in until all rice is covered.

4. Using tips of fingers, form rice in oval shape pressing firmly to hold rice together.

5. Place a slice of tuna over each rice mound and press lightly into rice.

6. Serve with wasabi past, ginger and soy sauce.

Nigiri Shrimp

Preparation time: 1 hour

Cooking Time: 30 minutes

Servings: 6

Ingredients:

Sushi rice, 3 1/3 cups

Water, 4 cups

Rice vinegar, 5 Tbsp.

Sugar, 3 Tbsp.

Salt, 1 tsp.

Shrimp, 6 oz., peeled and deveined and butterflied

Wasabi Paste, ½ cup

Pickled Ginger, ½ cup

Soy Sauce, ½ cup

Directions:

1. Wash rice under cold water until water runs clear.

2. Cook rice in rice cooker for 15 minutes. Let cool for 15 minutes.

3. Mix vinegar, sugar and salt. Sprinkle over rice and mix gently.

4. Wet fingertips and form rice into small oval mounds. Press firmly to help rice stick.

5. Lay a shrimp over each mound and press into rice gently.

6. Serve with wasabi paste, soy sauce and pickled ginger.

Nigiri Yellowtail Sushi

Preparation Time: 1 hour

Cooking Time: 25 to 30 minutes

Servings: 4

Ingredients:

Sushi Rice, 2 cups

Rice Vinegar, ½ cup

Sugar, 1 ½ Tbsp.

Salt, 1 ¼ tsp.

Yellowtail (Hamachi), 1 lb.

Eggs, 6

Wasabi Paste, 2 tsp.

Pickled Ginger, ½ cup

Soy Sauce, ½ cup

Directions:

1. Rinse rice in cold water.

2. Combine rice and water in rice cooker and cook for 20 minutes. Let stand for 10 minutes.

3. Combine rice vinegar, sugar and salt. Sprinkle over rice and coat.

4. Wet fingers and form mounds, pressing firmly.

5. Slice fish into thin strips and refrigerate.

6. Blend eggs, dash of sugar and salt. Pour ¼ of mixture into greased skillet. Let cook without stirring, about 5 minutes. Roll into logs. Continue with rest of egg mixture, forming logs to combine to make one large log. Then slice into ½ inch thick slices.

7. Form rice into oval mound.

8. Layer rice with egg and fish slice pressing gently.

9. Serve with wasabi paste, soy sauce and pickled ginger.

Tuna-Anchovy Nigiri-Sushi

Preparation Time: 45 minutes

Cooking Time: 20 minutes

Serves: 2

Ingredients:

Tuna, 1 can, drained

Anchovy, ½ cup, chopped

Sushi rice, 1 cup

Water, 1 cup

Rice Vinegar, 2 Tbsp.

Sugar, 1 Tsp.

Salt, 1 tsp.

Scallions, 2, chopped

Chives, ¼ cup, minced

Directions:

1. Rinse rice under cold water until water runs clear.

2. Cook rice in water in rice cooker for 20 minutes.

3. Mix rice vinegar, sugar and salt. Pour over rice and fold in.

4. Wet fingers and form rice patties, pressing lightly to form patties.

5. Add tuna, anchovies, scallions and chives on top.

6. Serve with pickled ginger, soy sauce and wasabi paste.

CHIRASHIZUSHI RECIPES (Scattered Sushi or Bowl Of Sushi)

Five-Flavor Chirashizushi

Preparation Time: 1 hour

Cooking Time: 30 minutes

Servings: 6

Ingredients:

Sushi Rice, 12 cups

Kampyo gourd, 5 ¼ oz.

Shitake Mushrooms, 3 ½ oz.

Carrots, 3 ½ oz.

Shirasu, 2 oz., dried

Conger eel, 3 ½ oz.

Stock, 6 Tbsp.

Mirin, 2 tsp.

Sugar, 3 tsp.

Sake, 3 tsp.

Soy Sauce, 3 tsp.

Nori sheets, 4

Lotus root, 3 ½ oz.

Snow Peas, 3 ½ oz.

Shredded thin omelet, made from 4 eggs

Soboro, 3 ½ oz.

Directions:

1. Slice gourd into strips along with the shitake mushrooms. Prepare sushi rice.

2. Fillet the eel and rub with salt.

3. Combine stock, mirin, sugar, sake and soy sauce and bring to boil.

4. Add the eel and boil for about 30 minutes. Remove and grill. Chop into small pieces.

5. Toast the nori sheets on both sides and crumble.

6. Drain all ingredients and mix with sushi rice.

7. Spoon rice in serving dishes and top with eel, lotus root, snow peas, omelet and soboro.

8. Servings will be lukewarm.

Tekka Sushi In A Bowl

Preparation Time: 30 minutes

Cooking Time: 20 minutes

Servings: 4

Ingredients:

Sushi Rice, 8 cups

Water, 7 cups

Rice Vinegar, 3 Tbsp.

Sugar, 2 Tbsp.

Salt, 1 tsp.

Tuna, 1 ¾ cups

Nori, 2 sheets

Wasabi Horseradish, 1 Tbsp.

Soy sauce, 2 Tbsp.

Pickled ginger, ¼ cup

Directions:

1. Rinse rice under cold water until water runs clear.

2. Combine rice and water and cook in rice cooker for 20 minutes.

3. Slice tuna and rub with wasabi horseradish and soy sauce.

4. Toast nori on both sides and flake.

5. Spoon sushi rice in bowls, sprinkle with nori flakes.

6. Fold tuna in half and place on top of sushi rice and nori.

7. Serve with wasabi horseradish, pickled ginger and soy sauce on the sides.

Salmon Chirashizushi

Preparation Time: 30 minutes

Cook Time: 20 minutes

Serves: 3

Ingredients:

Sushi Rice, 2 cups

Water, 2 cups

Rice Vinegar, 3 Tbsp.

Sugar, 2 Tbsp.

Salt, 1 ½ tsp.

Sesame Seeds, ½ cup

Nori Sheet, 1, shredded

Salmon, 1 Filet, salted

Cucumber, ½, sliced

Eggs, 2

Salmon Roe, ¼ cup

Shiso Leaves, 1 cup, chopped

Directions:

1. Place rice and in cooker and cook for 20 minutes. Let stand.

2. Combine rice vinegar, sugar, and salt. Pour over rice and mix.

3. Grill salmon, remove skin and bones, then flake.

4. Scramble eggs.

5. Prepare cucumber and shiso leaves.

6. Put sushi rice in bowl, top with sesame seeds, nori, cucumber, salmon, egg, salmon roe and shiso leaves.

7. Serve and enjoy.

Sushi With Squid And Red Caviar

Preparation Time: 60 minutes

Cooking Time: 20 minutes

Servings: 4

Ingredients:

Sushi Rice, 8 cups

Water, 8 cups

Squid, 1, cleaned, cut , salted

Sake, 1 Tbsp.

Salt, 1/3 tsp.

Sugar, ½ cup

Red Caviar, 5 Tbsp.

Trefoil, 1 ¼ oz.

Nori, 2 sheets

Wasabi Paste, ¼ cup

Pickled Ginger, ½ cup

Directions:

1. Cook rice and water in rice cooker for 20 minutes. Set aside.

2. Mix rice vinegar, sugar and salt. Pour over rice and blend lightly.

3. Prepare squid by rubbing with salt and sake. Toast lightly on both sides.

4. Toast nori sheets lightly. Then crush to make flakes.

5. Parboil the trefoil and sprinkle with soy sauce. Wash and cut into long pieces.

6. Put rice in bowl and top with nori flakes, squid, red caviar and trefoil.

7. Garnish with pickled ginger and wasabi paste.

8. Serve with sides of choice.

Scattered Yellowfin Rice Bowl

Preparation Time: 1 hour

Cooking Time: 45 minutes

Serves: 2

Ingredients:

Brown Rice, 1 cup, cooked

Water, 1 cup

Sesame Oil, 2 Tbsp.

Mirin, 1 ½ Tbsp.

Genmai Miso, 1 Tbsp.

Tamari, 2 tsps.

Fresh Ginger, 1 tsp., grated

Yellowfin fillets, 2

Oil, ¼ cup

Cucumber, ½ small, sliced

Carrot, ½ cup, shredded

Avocado, 1 small, sliced

Nori, ¼ sheet, toasted and shredded

Sesame Seeds, toasted, ¼ cup

Pickled Ginger, ½ cup

Directions:

1. Cook rice in rice cooker for 20 minutes. Let sit for 10 minutes.

2. Heat oil in skillet and cook fillets for 10 to 15 minutes.

3. Whisk sesame oil, mirin, genmai miso, tamari and fresh ginger until smooth.

4. Mix 1 Tbsp. Miso dressing mix with rice.

5. Add rice to bottom of bowl.

6. Arrange fish and vegetables over the rice.

7. Sprinkle nori and sesame seeds on top.

8. Sprinkle Miso dressing over rice, fish and vegetables.

9. Serve with pickled ginger.

Ocean Trout Sushi In A Bowl

Preparation Time: 60 minutes

Cooking Time: 30 minutes

Servings: 4

Ingredients:

Ocean Trout, 1 lb., Smoked

Carrot, 1

Green Beans, 1/3 bowl

Lotus root slices, 8 to 10

Mirin, 2 Tbsp.

Sugar, 1 Tbsp.

Rice, 2 cups, steamed

Soy based dressing, 1 Tbsp.

Hard Milked Caviar, 2 tsp.

Cooking Spray

Crepe mixture:

Eggs, 3

Sugar, 1 tsp.

Sake, 1 Tbsp.

Dashi, 1 Tbsp.

Water, 1 Tbsp.

Corn Starch, 1 tsp.

Salt, 1/4 tsp.

Directions:

1. *For The Crepe:* Whisk eggs, add sugar, sake, dashi, water, cornstarch and salt until smooth.

2. Spray skillet and heat. Pour thin layer and make a crepe. Remove pan from heat before it browns and let sit to finish cooking. Continue with rest of eggs to make crepes. Remove and cover.

3. When cool, cut crepes into noodles.

4. Simmer carrots, green beans and lotus roots in the sugar , mirin and soy until sugar has dissolved. About 10 minutes. Drain and set aside.

5. Steam rice in rice cooker, about 15 minutes.

6. Sprinkle soy based dressing over rice and combine.

7. Add vegetables to rice, add flaked trout on top, place crepe noodles on top.

8. Spoon caviar on top and serve.

Spicy Tuna & Avocado Chirashi

Preparation Time: 1 hour

Cooking Time: 30 minutes

Serves: 2

Ingredients:

Tuna, 6 oz., fresh, diced

Avocado, 1 large, diced

Sushi Rice, 1 cup

Water, 1 cup

Rice Vinegar, 1 tsp.

Japanese mayo, 4 Tbsp.

Sriracha Sauce, 2 Tbsp.

Radish sprouts, ½ cup

Directions:

1. Add rice and water to rice cooker and steam for 15 minutes.

2. Add rice vinegar to rice and fold in.

3. Place rice in each bowl, place tuna and avocado on top.

4. Sprinkle mayo and sriracha sauce.

5. Add radish sprouts for topping.

6. Serve at once.

INARIZUSHI RECIPES (Pouch of fried tofu (aburaage) filled with Sushi Rice)

Inarizushi (Shushi Tub)

Preparation Time: 60 minutes

Cooking Time: 30 minutes

Servings: 5

Ingredients:

Sushi Rice, 2 cups

Water, 2 cups

Tofu pouches, 10

Dashi, 2 tsp.

Soy Sauce, 2 Tbsp.

Sugar, 2 Tbsp.

Sake, 1 Tbsp.

Rice Vinegar, 1 Tbsp.

Sesame Seeds, 1 Tbsp.

Directions:

1. Cook rice in rice cooker for 15 minutes.

2. Meanwhile, boil some water in a pot. Place tofu pouches in boiling water and boil for 1 minute. Remove and let drain, discard the water. Cut a slit about 1/4 on the side of each pouch then pull open gently.

3. Add 1 1/2 cups of water to the pot and bring to a boil. Add dashi, sugar, soy sauce and sake to water and place tofu pouches back in. Simmer for 15 minutes. Remove tofu pouches and let drain.

4. Add rice vinegar and sesame seeds to rice, mix well. Wet fingers and pick up a handful of rice. Press together and place in tofu pouch.

6. Fold the ends over rice and serve.

Squid Inari Sushi

Preparation Time: 50 minutes

Cooking Time: 30 minutes

Servings: 4

Ingredients:

Sushi rice, 8 cups

Water, 7 cups

Rice vinegar, 2 Tbsp.

Sugar, 1 Tbsp.

Salt, 1 tsp.

Surimi Squid, 8 small

Mirin, 3 Tbsp.

Sake, 2 Tbsp.

Soy sauce, 4 Tbsp.

Shitake Mushroom, 4

Carrot, 1

Snow Peas, 1 oz., boiled

Sweet-sour pickled ginger stalks, 8

Directions:

1. Remove entrails, legs and thin outer skin from the squids.

2. Boil mirin, sake and soy sauce, add squid and cook for 20 to 30 minutes. Remove and set aside.

3. Prepare sushi rice in rice cooker with water.

4. Mix rice vinegar, sugar and salt. Blend in rice.

5. Mince mushrooms, carrots and snow peas and mix in rice.

6. Stuff squid with rice mixture.

7. Cut into slices. Brush with sauce.

8. Serve with pickled ginger stalks.

Soba Noodles Inarizushi

Preparation Time: 45 minutes

Cooking Time: 15 minutes

Servings: 2

Ingredients:

Aburaage, 10 sheets, seasoned

Dried Soba Noodles, 2 pkgs.

Cucumber, 1 diced

Naga-negi Onion, 6 inch

Okura, 3, boiled

Tempura bits, 2 Tbsp.

Wasabi, 2 Tbsp.

Mentsuyu, 2 Tbsp.

Sesame Oil, ½ Tbsp.

Sesame Seeds, Roasted, ½ cup

Directions:

1. Heat aburaage in hot water and squeeze liquid out.

2. Boil soba noodles and rinse in cold water.

3. Slice okura into rounds and chop the onions and cucumber into strips.

4. Mix mentsuyu, wasabi, and sesame oil. Blend in the okura, onions and cucumbers.

5. Add soba noodles and tempura and mix.

6. Fill the aburaage pockets and sprinkle with sesame seeds.

7. Serve with sides of your choice.

Kale, Mushroom and Water Chestnuts Inarizushi

Preparation Time: 30 minutes

Cooking Time: 15 minutes

Servings: 4

Ingredients:

Tofu pouches, 6, cooked

Brown Rice, 1 cup, cooked

Frozen peas, ¾ cup, cooked

Water, 1 cup

Carrots, 2, chopped

Kale, 1 bunch, stems removed and chopped

Dark sesame oil, ½ tsp.

Mushrooms, 12 oz., sliced

Ginger, 1 Tsp., minced

Garlic, 2 cloves, minced

Vegetable broth, ¼ cup

Water Chestnuts, 1 can, sliced, rinsed and drained

Ponzu, 3 Tbsp.

Rice Wine Vinegar, 1 Tsp.

Sugar, 1 Tsp.

Directions:

1. Add sesame oil to skillet and heat.

2. Add mushrooms, ginger and garlic and stir until tender.

3. Add kale and broth, cover and simmer for 10minutes, until kale is tender.

4. Remove cover and add water chestnuts. Simmer uncovered for 10 minutes.

5. Combine rice, rice vinegar, carrots and peas. Mix with kale mixture.

6. Form oblong mound of rice mixture with fingers and place in the inari pouches.

7. Serve with wasabi paste, pickled ginger and soy sauce.

Marinated Rice Inari Sushi

Preparation Time: 45 minutes

Cooking Time: 30 minutes

Servings: 4

Ingredients:

Sushi Rice, 1 ½ cup, uncooked

Water, 1 cup

Rice Vinegar, ¼ cup

Salt, ¾ tsp.

Sugar, 3 Tbsp.

Tofu Pouches, 1 pkg.

White sesame seeds, 1 ½ tsp.

Wasabi Paste, ¼ cup

Soy Sauce, ½ cup

Pickled ginger, ½ cup

Directions:

1. Prepare rice with water in rice cooker. Approximately 15 minutes. Let stand for 10 minutes.

2. Mix vinegar, salt and sugar. Blend with cooked rice.

3. Boil tofu pouches for 5 to 10 minutes.

4. Lightly toast sesame seeds for 5 minutes.

5. Open pouches and fill with seasoned rice.

6. Sprinkle with sesame seeds.

7. Serve with wasabi paste, soy sauce and pickled ginger.

OSHIZUSHI RECIPES (Pressed Sushi, Square Shaped Sushi)

Oshizushi Tuna Salad Sandwich

Preparation Time: 45 minutes

Cooking Time: 20 minutes

Servings: 2

Ingredients:

Tuna, 1 can, water packed, drained

Mayonnaise, 3 Tbsp.

Black Pepper, ¼ tsp.

Salt, ¼ tsp.

Sushi Rice, 1 cup

Rice vinegar, 2 Tbsp.

Water, 1 cup

Celery, 1 Tbsp., chopped

Directions:

1. Mix tuna, mayo, pepper and salt together. Set aside.

2. Cook rice in water, 20 minutes, set aside to cool then mix with rice vinegar.

3. Layer plastic wrap in square container.

4. Press rice onto plastic wrap.

5. Layer tuna salad on top of rice, sprinkle with capers and celery.

6. Place another layer of rice on top of tuna.

7. Use plastic to press firmly.

8. Store in refrigerator and slice as sandwich as needed.

Crab and Avocado Oshi Sushi

Preparation Time: 30 minutes

Cooking Time: 15 minutes

Serves: 2

Ingredients:

Oshibako, small box

Sushi Rice, 2 cups

Water, 2 cups

Rice Vinegar, 2 Tbsp.

Sugar, 2 Tbsp.

Salt, 1 tsp.

Crab Meat, 10 0z.

Avocado, 1 split, peeled and seed taken out, cut into thin slices

Wasabi-Mayo Sauce:

Mayonnaise (Japanese or Regular), 2 Tbsp.

Wasabi, 1 tsp

Directions:

1. Place mold in water and rice vinegar for 15 minutes.

2. Remove and dry.

3. Cook rice for 15 minutes. Let stand for 10 minutes.

4. Mix rice vinegar, salt and sugar. Add to rice and fold to mix.

5. Make wasabi mayo by mixing wasabi with mayonnaise in a bowl.

5. Place rice in mold, press with top.

6. Add a layer of wasabi mayo and spread evenly.

7. Add another layer of rice and press firmly.

8. Layer the crab meat and press lightly.

9. Slice in spaces of the box.

10. Remove box gradually.

11. Layer on plates and serve.

Sushi Napoleon

Preparation Time: 1 hour

Cooking Time: 20 minutes

Servings: 3

Ingredients:

Sushi Rice, 1 ½ cups, washed and drained

Water, 2 ½ cups

Rice vinegar, 1 Tbsp.

Sugar, 1 tsp.

Nori, 4 sheets

Asparagus Spears, 20

Cucumber, 1 sliced

Avocado, 1 whole, peeled, split, seed removed and sliced

Carrots, 1, shredded

Wasabi Sauce, ¼ cup

Teriyaki Sauce, ¼ cup

Sesame seeds, ¼ cup

Directions:

1. Cook rice with water in rice cooker for 20 minutes. Let sit for 10 minutes.

2. Blanch asparagus for 5 minutes. Cut off ends and set aside.

3. Combine rice vinegar, sugar and salt. Fold into rice.

4. Lay nori sheet on clean area and spread layer of rice, leaving an edge. Press firmly.

5. Press cucumbers on top of rice.

6. Spread another nori sheet with rice, turn over on top of cucumbers, keeping straight.

7. Press rice on top of nori sheet.

8. Layer asparagus on top of the second rice covered nori sheet. Add carrots among the asparagus.

9. Place rice on another nori sheet. Turn over and place on top of the carrots and asparagus.

10. Place another nori sheet on area and cover with rice. Add avocado layers. Turn sheet over on top of the other sheet to make even.

11. Cover with wax paper and press for 10 minutes to firm up the rice.

12. Wet knife and slice in 4 squares. Continue with other nori sheets and rice.

13. Serve with recommended sides.

SASHIMI

Salmon Sashimi with Ginger and Hot Sesame Oil

Preparation Time: 20 minutes

Cooking Time: 0

Servings: 4

Ingredients:

Soy Sauce, ¼ cup

Lime juice, 1 tsp.

Orange juice, 1 tsp.

Smoked Salmon, 12 slices, cut into squares

Ginger, 1, sliced thin

Chives, 1 Tbsp.

Grapeseed Oil, 2 Tbsp.

Sesame Oil, Roasted, 2 Tbsp.

Sesame Seeds, 1 ½ tsp.

Cilantro, 2 Tbsp., chopped

Directions:

1. Combine 2 Tbsp. of soy sauce, lime juice and orange juice.

2. Toss salmon with rest of soy sauce. Let stand. Drain and arrange 3 fillets on a plate.

3. Sprinkle with ginger and chives.

4. Heat grapeseed oil with sesame oil about 2 minutes.

5. Spoon oils over salmon. Drizzle soy/citrus sauce on top.

6. Add cilantro and sesame seeds on top and serve.

Ahi Poke Sashimi

Preparation Time: 8 minutes

Cooking Time: 0

Servings: 6

Ingredients:

Ahi Tuna Steaks, 2 large

Shallot, 1 sliced

Green Onion, ½ cup

Soy Sauce, 3 Tbsp.

Sesame Oil, 1 tsp.

Chili garlic sauce, 1 tsp.

Sesame seeds, 1 Tbsp.

Directions:

1. Dry the tuna steaks and cut into cubes.

2. Add shallots, green onion, soy sauce, sesame oil, garlic sauce and sesame seeds in bowl. Add tuna cubes and toss.

3. Serve immediately.

Kanpachi Sashimi

Preparation Time: 30 minutes

Cooking Time: 0

Servings: 2

Ingredients:

Daikon, 2 ½ oz., grated and drained

Sriracha, 1 tsp.

Soy Sauce, 1 Tbsp.

Yuzu juice, 1 Tbsp.

Kanpachi (yellowfin), 6 oz.

Chives, ¼ cup, chopped

Directions:

1.Combine drained daikon and sriracha. Mix well.

2. Mix soy sauce and yuzu juice to make ponzu.

3. Use a sashimi knife and slice the yellowfin into thin slices.

4. Place a dollop of spicy daikon on each slice of yellowfin.

5. Drizzle the ponzu on top of the fish and sprinkle with chives and serve.

Sashimi Cake

Preparation Time: 60 minutes

Cooking Time: 20 minutes

Servings: 6

Ingredients:

Sushi Rice, 1 ½ cup

Rice Vinegar, 12 Tbsp.

Sugar, 6 Tbsp.

Salt, 3 tsp.

Nori Sheet, 1

Salmon, 1 ¼ lb., skinless and boneless, diced

Avocado Oil, 2 Tbsp.

Cucumber, 1 large, diced

Avocado, 1 peeled, pitted and diced

Sesame Seeds, 4 Tbsp.

Directions:

1. Rinse rice and drain. Cook in rice cooker for 20 minutes. Let set for 10 minutes.

2. Mix rice vinegar, sugar and salt. Add to rice and fold in, coating well.

3. Combine diced salmon, sesame seeds and avocado oil. Set aside.

4. Place nori sheet in springform pan. Layer rice on top, pressing firmly.

5. Place diced cucumber and avocado on top of rice.

6. Placed diced salmon on top of cucumber.

7. Repeat layers and refrigerate until serving.

Sashimi with Soy Sauce, Sesame Seeds and Chives

Preparation Time: 20 minutes

Cooking Time: 20 minutes

Serves: 8

Ingredients:

Sushi Rice, 6 cups

Water, 6 cups

Rice Vinegar, ½ cup

Sugar, ¼ cup

Salt, 3 tsp.

Yellowfin Tuna, 1 lb. fresh, sliced

Extra-Virgin Olive Oil, 2 tsp.

Soy Sauce, 4 tsp.

White Sesame Seeds, 2 tsp.

Chives, ½ tsp. sliced thin

Directions:

1. Rinse rice with cold water and drain until clear.

2. Prepare rice in rice cooker with water and cook for 20 minutes. Set aside for 10 minutes.

3. Combine rice vinegar, sugar and salt. Sprinkle over rice and mix lightly. Add rice to 8 plates.

4. Arrange tuna slices and sprinkle with ¼ tsp. olive oil and ½ tsp. soy sauce.

5. Add sesame seeds and chives on top of tuna and serve.

6. Serve with soy sauce, wasabi and pickled ginger on the side.

SOUPS, SAUCES AND SALADS

Sushi Yum-Yum Sauce

Preparation Time: 15 minutes

Cooking Time: 1 hour

Servings: 6

Ingredients:

Mayonnaise, 1 cup

Rice vinegar, 3 Tbsp.

Sugar, 3 tsp.

Butter, 2 Tbsp., melted

Paprika, 3/8 tsp.

Garlic Powder, 3/8 tsp.

Directions:

1. Mix all ingredients together and whisk until smooth.

2. Refrigerate 1 hour before serving to enhance the flavors.

Ponzu Sauce

Preparation Time: 10 minutes

Cooking Time: 0

Servings: 4

Ingredients:

Green Onions, 1 Tbsp.

Lemon juice, 3 Tbsp.

Mirin, 2 Tbsp.

Soy Sauce, 2 Tbsp.

Brown Sugar, 1 tsp.

Red Pepper, ¼ tsp., crushed

Fish sauce, ¼ tsp.

Directions:

1. Mix all ingredients together and whisk to smooth.

2. Serve with different kinds of sushi.

Eel Sauce

Preparation Time: 5 minutes

Cooking Time: 5 minutes

Serves: 4

Ingredients:

Soy Sauce, 6 Tbsp.

Mirin, 4 Tbsp.

Brown Sugar, 2 Tbsp.

Rice vinegar, ½ tsp.

Directions:

1. Mix soy sauce, mirin, brown sugar and vinegar in small pan.

2. Bring to a boil and let boil for 1 minute. Reduce heat and simmer until thickened.

3. Set aside and let cool before serving.

Thai Dipping Sauce

Preparation Time: 10 minutes

Cooking Time: 0

Servings: 4

Ingredients:

Soy Sauce, 1/3 cup

Rice vinegar, 1/3 cup

Sriracha sauce, 1 tsp.

Sesame Oil, 1 tsp.

Ginger, 1 tsp.

Garlic, 2 cloves, minced

Scallions, 2, chopped.

Directions:

1. Mix all ingredients except scallions. Whisk.

2. Sprinkle with scallions before serving.

Spicy Sushi Sauce

Preparation Time: 5 minutes

Cooking Time: 0

Servings: 4

Ingredients:

Mayonnaise, ½ cup

Sriracha hot sauce, 2 Tbsp.

Roasted Sesame oil, ¼ tsp.

Directions:

1. Combine all ingredients and whisk.

2. Refrigerate until time to serve.

Miso Soup

Preparation Time: 5 minutes

Cooking Time: 10 minutes

Serves: 4 to 6

Ingredients:

Vegetable stock, 2 cups

Water, 2 cups

Soybean Paste, 4 Tbsp.

Soft Tofu, 12 oz. pkg., cubed

Nori, 6 sheets, cut into strips

Salt, ¼ tsp.

Scallions, 4, chopped

Directions:

1. Boil stock and water.

2. Add soybean paste and dissolve.

3. Simmer for 5 minutes, add tofu.

4. Add Nori strips and simmer 5 more minutes. Season with salt

5. Place in bowls, sprinkle with scallions and serve.

Crock Pot Japanese Onion Soup

Preparation Time: 30 minutes

Cooking Time: 4 hours

Servings: 6

Ingredients:

Carrots, 2 medium

Celery, 2 stalks

Garlic Cloves, 2, mashed

Chicken Broth, 6 cups

Onion, 1, wedged

Mushrooms, 8 oz., sliced

Green Onions, 4, chopped

Directions:

1. Place ingredients, minus mushrooms and green onions in crockpot.

2. Cover and cook on high for 4 hours.

3. Remove vegetables a little before done and add the mushrooms.

4. Cook for the rest of needed time, about 1 hour.

5. Spoon in bowls, top with green onions and serve.

Soba Noodle Soup

Preparation Time: 10 minutes

Cooking Time: 5 minutes

Servings: 1

Ingredients:

Soba noodles, 1 bunch

Water, 1 ½ cups

Bonito Flavored Soup Base, 2 Tbsp.

Shrimp, 3, shelled and deveined

Carrots, 3 slices

Snow peas, 3

Mushrooms, 3, sliced

Nori sheet, 1, cut into strips

Togarashi

Directions:

1. Boil the soba noodles about 5 minutes, then drain.

2. Bring water to a boil, add soup base and rest of ingredients.

3. Continue to boil for 1 minute until shrimp is cooked.

4. Serve over the noodles and sprinkle with nori and togarashi.

Beef Sukiyaki

Preparation Time: 45 minutes

Cooking Time: 15 minutes

Servings: 4

Ingredients:

Beef Fat Trimmings, 1 Tbsp.

Beef Strip Loin, 1 lb., sliced

Shallots, 8

Cabbage, ½ lb., sliced

Green Onions, 4, sliced

Shitake Mushrooms, 8, stems removed

Enoki Mushrooms, 7 oz., trimmed with stems removed

Broiled Tofu, ½ pkg., cut into sticks

Ito Konnyaku noodles, 7 oz., rinsed, drained and cut

Sake, 2 cups

Sugar, 1/3 cup

Soy Sauce, ½ cup

Arugula Leaves, 1 cup, rinsed and cut

Directions:

1. In cast iron skillet, heat fat trimmings. Add beef slices. Brown on each side.

2. Add shallots, cabbage, green onions, mushrooms, tofu and noodles.

3. Add sake sugar and soy sauce. Simmer for 10 minutes.

4. Add Arugula and cook for 1 minute.

5. Serve and enjoy.

Avocado, Crab and Brown Rice Sushi Salad

Preparation Time: 20 minutes

Cooking Time: 0

Servings: 6

Ingredients:

Rice vinegar, 1/3 cup

Sugar, 1 Tbsp.

Soy Sauce, 1 Tbsp.

Wasabi Paste, 2 tsp.

Sesame Oil, 2 tsp

Crab meat, 2 cans chunked, drained

Carrot, 1, cut into matchsticks

Japanese cucumber, 1, sliced thin

Green Onions, 3, sliced thin diagonally

Pickled ginger, 3 Tbsp., chopped

Sesame Seeds, 1 Tbsp.

Brown Rice, 1 ½ cups, cooked

Avocado, 1, peeled, pitted and sliced

Nori, 1 toasted and cut into strips

Directions:

1. Combine 4 Tbsp. vinegar, sugar and soy sauce.

2. Pour over cooked rice and toss.

3. Combine rest of vinegar, wasabi and sesame oil. Set aside.

4. Combine crab, carrot, cucumber, onions, pickled ginger and sesame seeds with rice. Pour wasabi mixture over and mix.

5. Add avocado strips and sprinkle with nori strips.

6. Serve cold.

Ahi Tuna Sushi Salad

Preparation Time: 10 minutes

Cooking Time: 10 minutes

Servings: 4

Ingredients:

Wasabi paste, 1 tsp.

Rice vinegar, 2 Tbsp.

Oil, 3 Tbsp.

Soy Sauce, 1 Tbsp.

Mirin, 1 Tbsp.

Ginger, 1 Tsp., grated

Ahi Tuna, 1 lb.

Black Sesame seeds, 2 Tbsp.

White Sesame seeds, 2 Tbsp.

Salad Greens, 6 cups

Avocado, 1 large, sliced

Cucumber, 1 cup sliced

Carrot, ½ cup, shredded

Edamame, ½ cup

Green Onions, 2, sliced

Pickled ginger, 2 Tbsp.

Directions:

1. Mix wasabi paste, vinegar, 2 Tbsp. oil, soy sauce, mirin and ginger together for the vinaigrette.

2. Heat 1 Tbsp. oil over medium heat.

3. Roll tuna in sesame seeds and press into the tuna. Sear the tuna 2 minutes on each side. Set aside and slice.

4. Combine salad greens with avocado, cucumber, carrot, edamame, green onions and pickled ginger. Toss well.

5. Place ahi tuna over salad, toss.

6. Add vinaigrette before serving.

Spicy Sushi Salad

Preparation Time: 45 minute

Cooking Time: 20

Serves: 4

Ingredients:

Sushi Rice, 2 cups

Water, 2 cups

Rice Vinegar, 1 ½ tsp.

Sugar, 2 Tbsp.

Salt, 2 tsp.

Tuna, 4 oz., diced

Black Pepper, 3 tsp.

Avocado, 1, sliced

Snow Crab, 4 oz.

Sesame Seeds, 1 Tbsp.

Nori, 1 sheet, crumbled

Mayo, 1 Tbsp.

Sriracha, 1 tsp.

Directions:

1. Rinse rice in cold water and drain.

2. Cook rice with water in rice cooker for 20 minutes.

3. Mix vinegar, sugar and salt. Pour over rice and toss.

4. Combine tuna with pepper.

5. Combine mayo and sriracha and stir well.

6. Spread sushi rice on plate, add tuna and avocado slices.

7. Add crab meat. Sprinkle with sesame seeds and Nori.

8. Serve with sriracha mayo on top.

Kani Salad

Preparation Time: 10 minutes

Cooking Time: 3 minutes

Servings: 2

Ingredients:

Cucumber, 1, cut into strips

Salt, ½ tsp.

Glass Noodles, 1 pkg.

Crab, 1 can, drained

Mayonnaise, 3 Tbsp.

Lime, ½

Directions:

1. Boil water in pot. Add noodles and cook for 3 minutes. Drain and rinse with cold water.

2. Add crab to noodles.

3. Mix cucumbers with salt and toss to coat. Squeeze liquid out of cucumbers.

4. Add cucumbers to crab and noodles.

5. Add mayonnaise and lime juice. Stir well.

6. Serve cold.

Sushi Seaweed Salad

Preparation Time: 30 minutes

Cooking Time: 0

Serves: 1

Ingredients:

Dried seaweed, 1 oz.

Scallions, ¼ cup, minced

Soy Sauce, 2 Tbsp.

Mirin, 1 tsp.

Dark sesame oil, ½ tsp.

Cayenne salt, 1 pinch

Sesame seeds, 1 Tbsp., toasted

Directions:

1. Rinse seaweed and soak about 5 minutes to increase the size.

2. Gently squeeze and place in bowl.

3. Mix scallions, soy sauce, mirin, sesame oil and cayenne salt. Toss to coat.

4. Sprinkle with sesame seeds and serve.

POPULAR WESTERN SUSHI

California Roll Sushi Salad

Preparation Time: 30 minutes

Cooking Time: 0

Servings: 4

Ingredients:

Spinach, 4 cups, torn

Cauliflower, 1 med. Head, shredded

Cucumber, 1 cup, diced

Carrot, ½ cup, shredded

Avocado, 1, pitted, diced

Crab Meat, 1 can, drained

Seaweed Snack Chips, 10, in pieces

Sesame Seeds, 1 Tbsp., toasted

Dressing:

Wasabi paste, 1 tsp.

Soy Sauce, 1 Tbsp.

Rice Vinegar, 2 Tbsp.

Sugar, ½ cup

Sesame oil, ½ tsp.

Directions:

1. Combine wasabi paste, soy sauce, vinegar, sugar and sesame oil.

2. Place spinach on plates.

3. Top with seaweed chips, cauliflower, cucumber, carrot, avocado and crab meat.

4. Add dressing, sprinkle with sesame seeds and serve.

Western Style Sushi

Preparation Time: 60 minutes

Cooking Time: 30 minutes

Servings: 2

Ingredients:

White Rice, 1 ½ cup

Water, 1 cup

Vinegar, 1 ½ Tbsp.

Sugar, 1 tsp.

Salt, ¼ tsp.

Sweet Onion, ¼, diced

Prosciutto, 6 slices

Cream Cheese, 8 oz.

Tomatos, diced

Cucumber, diced

Olive Oil, 2 Tbsp.

Directions:

1. Rinse rice in cold water and drain well.

2. Cook rice with water in rice cooker for 20 minutes.

3. Mix vinegar, sugar and salt. Set aside.

4. Cut prosciutto in half and dice the cream cheese.

5. Spoon rice in bowl, add sushi vinegar and onion. Mix well.

6. Place ham, cream cheese and rice in order on plastic wrap. Twist into a ball.

7. Finish with more balls.

8. Line on plate and top with tomato and cucumber. Drizzle with olive oil.

9. Serve with dips of choice.

Cowboy Sushi

Preparation Time: 45 minutes

Cooking Time: 0

Serves: 4

Ingredients:

Cooked Ham, 1 pkg.

Cream Cheese, 8 oz.

Kosher Dill Pickles, 1 jar

Pickled Okra, 1 jar

Directions:

1. Dry ham on both sides with paper towel. Spread ham with cream cheese. Repeat.

2. Dry pickles, one at a time. Roll ham around pickle. Place in refrigerator for 20 minutes, then slice into bite sizes.

3. Repeat with okra.

4. Arrange on platter and serve.

Western Style Eel Roll

Preparation Time: 60 minutes

Cook Time: 30 minutes

Serves: 2

Ingredients:

Nori Sheet, 1, cut into half

Sushi Rice, 1 cup, prepared ahead of time

Cream Cheese, ¼ of block, cut into strips

Cucumbers, 2, sliced

Unagi, 6 oz., cooked, cut into strips

Sesame Seeds, ¼ cup

Eel Sauce, ¼ cup

Directions:

1. Toast eel at 300F 5 minutes, then cut into strips.

2. Lay Nori on bamboo mat and spread sushi rice, pressing firmly.

3. Add the Unagi, cream cheese and cucumber.

4. Roll tightly, pressing as you go.

5. Unroll the eel roll and sprinkle with sesame seeds.

6. Slice and dip in eel sauce.

Frushi Sushi

Preparation Time: 45 minutes

Cooking Time: 20 minutes

Servings: 6

Ingredients:

Sushi Rice, 2 cups

Water, 2 cups

Cream of Coconut, 1 Tbsp.

Soy wrappers, 16

Strawberries, 16

Cantaloupe, ½ , rectangeled

Pineapple, 1/2 peeled and cored, rectangular

Toasted coconut, ½ cup

Directions:

1. Rinse rice under cold water and drain.

2. Cook rice with water in rice cooker for 20 minutes.

3. Mix rice with cream of coconut.

4. Place soy wrapper on working area and add rice on the wrapper, pressing firmly.

5. Add a piece of pineapple and cantaloupe. Add 4 slices of strawberries.

6. Roll soy wrapper, moisten and seal.

7. Slice into 4 pieces. Finish with remaining ingredients.

8. Sprinkle with toasted coconut and serve.

LATIN, MEDITERRANEAN & CARIBBEAN SUSHI

Latin Style Wontons

Preparation Time: 30 minutes

Cooking Time: 5 minutes

Serves: 2

Ingredients:

Ginger, 2 Tbsp., minced

Garlic, 1 clove, minced

Carrot, 1 shredded

Cilantro, 2 Tbsp., minced

Lemon juice of 1 lemon

Shallot, 1 chopped

Chives, 2 Tbsp., chopped

Shrimp, 1 lb., peeled and deveined

Olive Oil Mayo, 2 Tbsp.

Egg, 1 beaten

Oil, ¼ cup

Wonton wrappers, 20

Directions:

1. Mix ginger, shallot, garlic, carrots, cilantro, olive oil mayo, lemon juice, chives and shrimp.

2. Season with salt and pepper.

3. Place wonton on surface and brush on egg.

4. Place 1 spoonful of mixture on wonton. Close the ends of the wonton and press to seal.

5. Heat oil in skillet and fry for 5 minutes until done.

6. Serve alone or with dip.

Salmon Plantains and Pineapple

Preparation Time: 10 minutes

Cooking Time: 25 minutes

Servings: 4

Ingredients:

Salmon, 1 lb., cut into 4 fillets

Plantains, 2, very ripe

Pineapple Rings, 4

Maple Syrup, 2 Tbsp.

Balsamic Vinegar, 2 Tbsp.

Soy Sauce, 1 Tbsp.

Salt, ¼ tsp.

Pepper, ¼ tsp.

Red Onion, ¼, chopped

Lime, juice from 1

Cilantro, 1 Tbsp., minced

Olive Oil, 1 Tbsp.

Directions:

1. Preheat oven to 450F. Line pan with foil and rub with olive oil.

2. Peel and slice plantains into slices and place on pan. Place pineapple slices on pan also.

3. Combine maple syrup, balsamic vinegar and soy sauce. Brush plantains and pineapple.

4. Bake for 15 minutes. Turn halfway through.

5. Remove plantains and pineapples.

6. Place salmon on pan and cook for 10 minutes.

7. Cut pineapple into pieces, add to cilantro and onion. Add lime juice and toss. Season with salt and pepper.

8. When salmon is done place pineapple and plantains on top and serve.

Latin American Ceviche

Preparation Time: 15 minutes

Cooking Time: 0

Servings: 4

Ingredients:

Red Snapper fillets, 2 lbs., cut into pieces

Lime juice, ½ cup

Lemon juice, ½ cup

Red Onion, ½ diced

Tomatoes, 1 cup, diced

Serrano Chili, seeded and diced

Salt, 2 tsp.

Oregano, ¼ tsp.

Cayenne Pepper, ¼ tsp.

Cilantro, ¼ cup, minced

Tortillas, 4

Directions:

1. Combine fish, onion, tomatoes, chili, salt, cayenne pepper and oregano. Add lime and lemon juice. Cover and refrigerate for 1 hour.

2. Remove and serve with cilantro and tortillas.

Causushi

Preparation Time: 30 minutes

Cooking Time: 0

Serves: 2

Ingredients:

Causa, potato dough, 1 pkg.

Nori sheets, 1

Crabmeat, 8 oz., cooked

Mayonnaise, 2 cups

Worcestershire sauce, 2 Tbsp.

Lemon, juice from 1

Salt, ¼ tsp.

Pepper, ¼ tsp.

Aji Amarillo paste, 1 Tbsp.

Directions:

1. Spread a layer of causa on parchment sheet, place nori on top.

2. Mix crabmeat, Worcestershire sauce, 1 cup mayo, lemon juice, salt and pepper.

3. Roll as you would a sushi roll. Cut into 1-inch pieces.

4. Mix 1 cup mayo, Amarillo paste, salt and pepper. Set aside.

5. Place pieces on plate and serve with chili sauce mixture.

Escabeche

Preparation Time: 60 minutes

Cooking Time: 30 minutes

Servings: 2

Ingredients:

Mackerel, 1 whole fish

Salt, 1 tsp.

Pepper, 1 tsp.

Flour, ¼ cup

Garlic, 1 tsp., minced

Ginger Root, 1 Tbsp.

Onions, ½ cup, sliced

Red and green bell peppers, 1 cup, cut into strips

Oil, 2 Tbsp.

Water, 2 cups

Vinegar, ¼ cup

Brown Sugar, ¼ cup

Soy sauce, 2 Tbsp.

Cornstarch, 2 Tbsp.

Directions:

1. Salt and pepper the fish and rub in.

2. Dredge with flour and deep fry.

3. Add oil to skillet and sauté garlic, ginger, onions and bell peppers until tender.

4. Mix water, vinegar, sugar, soy sauce, cornstarch, salt and pepper. Simmer for 5 minutes.

5. Add fish to platter and add sauce on top.

6. Sprinkle ginger, onions and peppers on top and serve.

Mediterranean Sushi

Preparation Time: 45 minutes

Cooking Time: 20 minutes

Serves: 4

Ingredients:

Nori sheets, 4

White Rice, 4 Cups

Water, 3 ½ cups

Rice Vinegar, 2 Tbsp.

Mirin, 1 Tbsp.

Sugar, 1 tsp.

Salt, 1 tsp.

Avocado, 1, peeled, pitted and sliced

Red Pepper, 1, deseeded and sliced

Yellow Pepper, 1, deseeded and sliced

Feta Cheese, 1 cup

Directions:

1. Cook rice in water in rice cooker for 20 minutes.

2. Mix vinegar, mirin, sugar and salt. Mix well with rice.

3. Lay nori sheet on mat. Spread with rice.

4. Lay a slice of avocado and a slice of each color pepper in the middle of sheet.

5. Sprinkle with feta cheese.

6. Roll and press firmly as rolling to form roll.

7. Slice in 1 inch segments.

8. Serve with sweet chili sauce, soy sauce and wasabi.

Mediterranean Pressed Sushi

Preparation Time: 45 minutes

Cooking Time: 20 minutes

Servings: 2

Ingredients:

Sushi Rice, 1 cup

Water, ¾ cup

Seaweed, ½ lb.

Rice seasoning, 1 Tbsp.

Mozzarella Cheese, ¾ cup

Red Bell Peppers, 1, sliced

Sun-dried Tomatoes, 4

Basil Leaves, 2

Oil, 1 Tbsp.

Directions:

1. Rinse rice under cold water until water runs clear.

2. Combine rice and water in rice cooker and cook for 20 minutes.

3. Arrange rice in bowl and add rice seasoning. Mix well with hands.

4. Preheat oven 200F. Add bell peppers to pan and roast for 5 minutes. Pull skin off when cool and cut into strips.

5. Drain tomatoes and cut into strips.

6. Dice basil leaves.

7. Slice mozzarella cheese thinly.

8. Oil pan. Layer rice, oil top of rice, spread bell pepper and mozzarella cheese.

9. Cool in refrigerator for 15 to 20 minutes.

10. Remove and slice. Place tomato slice and basil on top and serve.

Tuna Tartare Sushi

Preparation Time: 10 minutes

Cooking Time: 0

Servings: 4

Ingredients:

Sushi grade Tuna, 14 oz.

Mint, 1 bunch

Lemons, 2

Sea Salt, ¼ tsp.

Olive Oil, 1 tsp.

Directions:

1. Chop tuna and add zest of 1 lemon. Chop the mint and add to tuna. Sprinkle some salt to taste.

2. Place on plate with lemon slices and drizzle with olive oil.

3. Prepare 4 servings.

Vegetarian Mediterranean Sushi

Preparation Time: 30 minutes

Cooking Time: 0

Servings: 2

Ingredients:

Cucumber, 1

Feta Cheese, ¾ cup

Roasted garlic hummus, ½ cup

Red Pepper, ¼, diced

Directions:

1. Use a vegetable peeler to make long strips out of your cucumber. Place cumber peels on platter.

2. Add hummus onto cucumber strips.

4. Add red pepper and feta cheese.

5. Roll up cucumber peels and place on plate.

Iberico Ham Sushi Roll

Preparation Time: 40 minutes

Cooking Time: 0

Servings: 2

Ingredients:

Sushi Rice, 1 1/3 cup, cooked

Nori Sheet, 1

Iberico Ham, 3 pkgs.

Mozzarella Cheese, 7 oz.

Eggs, 2

Wheat Flour, ½ cup

Panko Bread Crumbs, 7/8 cup

Olive Oil

Arugula, 3 ½ oz.

Basil Leaves, 2

Alfalfa Sprouts, ¼ cup

Pea Sprouts, ½ cup

Capers, ¼ cup

For Tomato Sauce:

Dried Tomatoes, 2 oz.

Lime juice, 2 tsp.

Olive Oil, 4 tsp.

Salt, ¼ tsp.

Pepper, ¼ tsp.

Directions:

1. Slice cheese into sticks.

2. Beat eggs with whisk.

3. Roll cheese sticks in flour and dip in egg.

4. Roll cheese sticks in panko crumbs.

5. Heat oil and fry sticks, drain.

6. Blend tomatoes, lime juice, olive oil, salt, capers and pepper.

7. Divide nori sheet into two sheets.

8. Layer rice on each sheet. Place ham slice on rice. Divide tomatoes onto both sheets. Place cheese sticks on each sheet.

9. Sprinkle with arugula, basil leaves and sprouts.

10. Place a slice of ham on top.

11. Roll firmly and slice. Add a caper on top of each slice.

12. Serve with tomato sauce.

Mediterranean Tortilla Sushi

Preparation Time: 20 minutes

Cooking Time: 0

Servings: 2

Ingredients:

Tortillas, 4, 6-inch

Greek Olive Hummus, ½ cup

Capicollo, 20 slices

Smoked Ham, 4 slices

Red Pepper, 1, cut into strips

Zucchini, 2, cut into strips

Mediterranean Microgreens, 1 cup

Directions:

1. Lay tortillas on work surface. Spread each with 2 tablespoons of hummus.

2. Layer with capicollo, ham slices, red pepper, zucchini and microgreens.

3. Roll up tortillas and slice into bite size pieces.

Caribbean Mango Avocado Ahi Lettuce Sushi

Preparation Time: 10 minutes

Cooking Time: 0

Serves: 4

Ingredients:

Mango, 1, diced

Avocado, 1, peeled, pitted and diced

Red Onion, ½ , diced

Ahi Tuna, ½ lb., diced

Lime, 1

Olive Oil, 1 Tbsp.

Cilantro, 1 Tbsp.

Pepper, ¼ tsp.

Butter lettuce, 1 head

Directions:

1. Mix mango, avocado, onion and ahi.

2. Squeeze the juice of 1 lime over mixture. Sprinkle olive oil over mixture also.

3. Add cilantro and pepper on top.

5. Mix and spoon in middle of 2 lettuce leaves.

6. Roll tight and serve.

Caribbean Nori Chicken

Preparation Time: 1 hour

Cooking Time: 40 minutes

Serves: 4

Ingredients:

Chicken, 1 lb, chunked

Oil, 1 cup

Mochiko Flour,1 Tbsp.

Sugar, 1 Tbsp.

Cornstarch, 1 Tbsp.

Salt, 1 tsp.

Soy Sauce, 2 Tbsp.

Egg, 1

Garlic, 2 cloves

Green Onions, 4 diced

Nori Sheets, 2, cut into strips

Directions:

1. Mix chicken, flour, sugar, cornstarch, salt, soy sauce, egg, and green onions. Marinate 2 hours.

2. Wrap each chicken with a strip of nori sheet.

3. Fry until browned.

Caribbean Style Squid Ceviche

Preparation Time: 30 minutes

Cook Time: 10 minutes

Servings: 4

Ingredients:

Squid, 1 lb., cut into rings

Lime Juice, 3 Tbsp.

Sunflower Oil, 1 Tbsp.

Vinegar, 1 Tbsp.

Coriander Leaves, 4 Tbsp.

Serrano Chilies, 2, minced

Sugar, 1 tsp.

Red Onion, 1, minced

Garlic, 1, clove, halved

Salt, ¼ tsp

Pepper, ¼ tsp.

Directions:

1. Blend lime juice, sunflower oil, vinegar, coriander leaves, chilies, sugar, onion, garlic, salt and pepper.

2. Wash squid. Bring pot of water to a boil.

3. Blanch squid for one minute. Place squid in cold water.

4. Add squid to mixture and marinade for 1 hour.

5. Place in glass and serve cold.

Mango Sauce

Preparation Time: 15 minutes

Cooking Time: 0

Serves: 2

Ingredients:

Mangos, 2, ripe

Soy Sauce, 2 Tbsp.

Coconut milk, 4 Tbsp.

Thai chili sauce, 2 Tbsp.

Brown Sugar, 2 Tbsp.

Garlic, 3 cloves, minced

Lime juice, 1 Tbsp.

Turmeric, ¼ tsp.

Crushed chili, ¼ tsp.

Directions:

1. Scoop out mangos and blend well.

2. Add soy sauce, milk, chili sauce, brown sugar, garlic, lime juice, turmeric and crushed chili.

3. Blend until smooth.

4. Divide and serve with Caribbean sushi.

Caribbean Salmon Sushi Bites

Preparation Time: 15 minutes

Cooking Time: 0

Servings: 4

Ingredients:

Salmon, 2 fillets, cut into bite-sized pieces

Nori Sheets, 2, cut into bite-sized squares, roasted

Green onions, 3, diced

Mango, ½, diced

Directions:

1. Arrange nori sheets on tray.

2. Place salmon bites on sheets.

3. Top with green onions and mango pieces.

4. Serve as an appetizer.

Caribbean Ahi Tuna Sushi Bites

Preparation Time: 10 minutes

Cooking Time: 5

Servings: 6

Ingredients:

Ahi Tuna, 1 lb.

Vegetable Oil, 1 Tbsp.

Blackening Season, 1 Tbsp.

Mayonnaise, ½ cup

Wasabi, 2 Tbsp.

Cucumber, 1, cut into slices

Pickled Ginger, ½ cup

Directions:

1. Combine mayo and wasabi.

2. Rub blackening season on tuna.

3. Heat oil in skillet and sear tuna on both sides. Remove and cut into bite size pieces.

4. Spread mayo mixture on each cucumber slice. Top with ahi tuna and pickled ginger.

5. Serve cold.

END

Thank you for reading my book. If you enjoyed it, won't you please take a moment to leave me a good review at your retailer?

Thanks!

Kristen Barton

Made in the USA
San Bernardino, CA
29 May 2016